W

Po

OCR Gateway A Chemistry 1, 2 and 3

For GCSE Combined Science Higher Tier

NAFEESA ALAM

For all my students who have given me the motivation to keep trying new techniques and who let me know the time spent on them was appreciated.

Subscribe to Wright Science on YouTube to for a full set of videos to support you in your GCSE science studies.

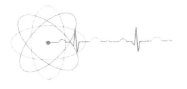

WRIGHT SCIENCE
SCIENCE DONE THE WRIGHT WAY

ISBN-13: 9781091468375

C1
Particles

C1.1.1: Particles

Everything is made from matter and matter is made from particles.

Models are used to solve problems, make predictions and develop scientific understanding.

The particle model describes the arrangement of particles and their movement in the different states of matter.

The particle model can be used to explain certain properties of a substance:
- You can compress gases as there is space between the particles but not liquids or solids.
- Solids cannot flow as they are arranged in a fixed shape.

State	Diagram	Movement of particles
Solid		Vibrate around fixed positions
Liquid		Move around each other
Gas		Move quickly in all directions

When we draw particles in a 3D diagram, certain particles are hidden from view either partially or fully.

C1.1.2: Chemical and Physical Changes

There are two types of change that can occur:

1) Physical change – Change in the state of matter e.g. melting or dissolving
These tend to be reversible and no new substance is made.
The particles stay the same but their arrangement and movement changes.

2) Chemical change – A change that produces one or more new substances.
These tend to be irreversible and the properties of the products are often very different to that of the reactants.
The particles break apart and join together in different ways.

C1.1.3: Limitations of the Particle Model

A typical atom has a radius of approximately 10^{-10}m or 0.1nm. This is the same size as a typical bond length.

Particles are held together by electrostatic forces of attraction. These occur between positive and negative charges. The further apart the particles are, the weaker the forces.

The particle model has some limitations as it does not take the following into account:
- Forces between particles
- Size of particles
- Space between particles

Check Your Understanding

1. Describe the arrangement of particles in a solid.

2. Compare the arrangement of particles in a liquid and a gas.

3. Explain what is meant by the term physical change.

4. Explain what is meant by the term chemical change.

5. List three limitations of the particle model.

6. State the size of a typical atom.

C1.2.1: Atomic Structure

Element: Substance whose atoms have the same atomic number.

Atom: Smallest particle of an element.

Molecule: Particle consisting of two or more atoms chemically joined by bonds.

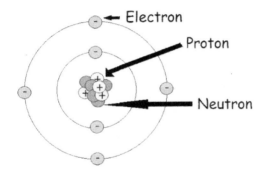

An atom is made from three subatomic particles – Protons, neutrons and electrons. The protons and neutrons are found in the nucleus. The electrons surround the nucleus in shells.

Subatomic Particle	Relative Mass	Relative Charge
Proton	1	+1
Neutron	1	0
Electron	0.0005	-1

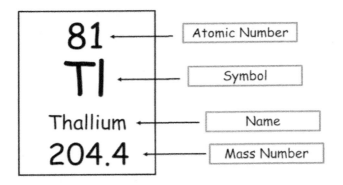

Atomic Number: The number of protons OR electrons.

Mass Number: The number of protons + neutrons.

Isotope: Element with the same number of protons and electrons but a different number of neutrons. Atomic number is the same but the mass number is different.

Ion: Charged particle.

To work out how many electrons or protons are in an atom, we just write down the atomic number from the periodic table.

To work out how many neutrons are present, subtract the atomic number from the mass number.

For an ion to form, electron(s) are either gained or lost by the atom.
If electron(s) are gained, the ion will have a negative charge.
If electron(s) are lost, the ion will have a positive charge.

C1.2.3: Developing the Atomic Model

The model of the atom has changed over time as new discoveries were made and new technology was developed.

John Dalton, 1803

All matter is made from atoms.
All atoms of an element are identical.
Different elements contain different types of atom.
Atoms are tiny, indestructible spheres.

J.J. Thomson, 1897

Discovered the electron in his cathode ray experiments. He found the beams changed direction in magnetic or electric fields so he concluded the cathode rays were tiny negative particles – electrons.

His model was called the plum-pudding model.

Ernest Rutherford with Geiger and Marsden, 1909

Fired beams of positively charged alpha particles at thin sheets of gold foil.
If plum-pudding was correct, the alpha particles would have passed straight through.
They found that many changed direction suggestion something was stopping them passing through.

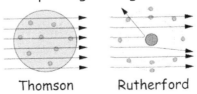

Thomson   Rutherford

Rutherford explained this by suggesting the atom has a positive nucleus and the electrons orbit it like planets around our Sun.

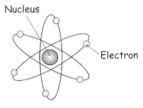

Nucleus

Electron

Niels Bohr, 1913

Showed that electrons occupy fixed energy levels around the nucleus.

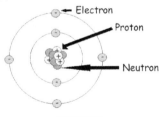

Electron

Proton

Neutron

Check Your Understanding

1. Describe the structure of an atom.

2. State the relative charge and relative mass of the three subatomic particles.

3. Define the term isotope.

4. Explain how to work out the number of protons in an atom.

5. Explain how to work out the number of neutrons in an atom.

6. Explain how an ion formed.

7. Describe how ideas about atoms have changed over time with reference to the scientists and their contributions.

C2
Elements, compounds and mixtures

C2.1.1: Relative Formula Mass

When talking about subatomic particles, we use the relative mass which is compared to the mass of a proton.

The relative atomic mass, A_r, is the mean mass of an atom of an element compared to 1/12th the mass of an atom of carbon-12.

We use relative masses as if we used grams, the numbers would be to many decimal places and be tricky to use.

When you look at a chemical formula, you can reveal information about the chemical. E.g. H_2SO_4

There are three different elements: Oxygen, hydrogen and sulphur. There are seven atoms: 2 hydrogen, 1 sulphur and 4 oxygen. It is a compound.

The rules for chemical formulae:
1. Capital letters show a new element.
2. The number to the bottom right of a symbol tells you the number of that element present.
3. A number in front of the formula tells you there are that many molecules.
4. A number after brackets tells you to multiply everything inside the bracket by that number. E.g. $Ca(OH)_2$ – 1 x Calcium; 2 x oxygen; 2 x hydrogen

When you have a chemical formula, you can calculate the relative formula mass, M_r.

To do this, you just need to add up all the relative atomic masses.

E.g. $Mg(OH)_2$

1. Write down the A_r for each element: Mg = 24.3; O = 16.0   H = 1.0
2. Work out the number of atoms of each element: Mg = 1; O = 2; H =2
3. Multiply the A_r by number and add them together: $(1 \times 24.2) + (2 \times 16.0) + (2 \times 1.0)$ = 58.3

The M_r of all reactants must equal to M_r of all products as atoms cannot be created or destroyed.

C1.1.2: Empirical Formula

The empirical formula shows the simplest whole number ratio of the atoms of each element in a compound.

To work this out:

1. Find the highest common factor (HCF) for all the elements in the formula.
C_4H_{10} has the HCF of 2.
2. Divide the chemical formula by the HCF.
C: $4 \div 2 = 2$
H: $10 \div 2 = 5$
3. Write the empirical formula.
C_2H_5

C2.1.3: Pure and Impure Substances

Pure: Substance that consists of one element or compound.
Impure: Substance that contains more than one element or compound.
Mixture: More than one element or compound mixed together but NOT chemically bonded.
Alloy: Mixture of a metal with one or more other elements.

We can use the melting point to determine if a substance is pure or not. A pure substance will have a single temperature melting point.
Impure substances will melt over a range of temperatures and melt at a lower temperature than the pure substance.

We can determine the melting point by heating it and recording the temperature it melts at. When doing this, you must heat the substance slowly to allow the temperature of the whole substance to increase and stir it to ensure the whole sample is at the right temperature.

C2.1.4: Filtration and Crystallisation (& PAG C3)

Solution: solute dissolved in the solvent

Solvent: Liquid that dissolves the solute

Solute: Solid that dissolves in the solvent

Soluble: Substance that will dissolve

Insoluble: Substance that will not dissolve

When a substance dissolves, its particles separate and become completely mixed with the particles of the solvent. Remember, not all substances dissolve in all solvents.

Filtration

Used to separate an insoluble solid from a liquid.

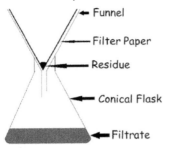

Filter paper has microscopic holes in it. These holes allow the small molecules to pass through but not larger ones. So the larger particles stay in the filter paper as the residue and the smaller particles pass through as the filtrate.

Crystallisation

Used to separate a dissolved substance from a solution.

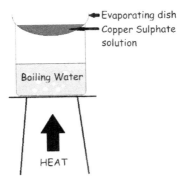

Crystallisation requires the solution to be heated gently until it becomes saturated. At this point, crystals will form. As the solution cools, the solubility of the solute decreases so more crystals form.

Saturated solution: Solution where no more solute can dissolve at that temperature.

Filtration can then be used to separate the crystals from the remaining solution. The crystals are then dried in a warm oven.

C2.1.5: Distillation (& PAG C4)

Simple distillation is used to separate a solvent from a solution.

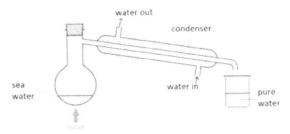

The key point to remember is that the solvent must have a lower boiling point than the solute. This means the solvent will evaporate before the solute. The solvent vapour is then cooled in the condenser to condense the vapour to a liquid for collection.

Fractional distillation is used to separate
two or more substances from a mixture in
the liquid state. This will only work if each
substance has a different boiling point.

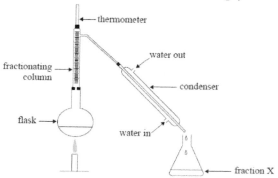

As the mixture of liquids is heated, the
one with the lowest boiling point
evaporates first. The vapour travels up
the fractionating column and passes into
the condenser which makes the vapour
condense to a liquid which can be collected.

C2.1.6: Chromatography (& PAG C3)

Used to separate mixtures of inks or dyes.

Chromatography relies on two chemical phases:
1) Stationary phase – Does not move
2) Mobile phase – Moves

There are two types of chromatography we could use:
1) Thin-layer chromatography – Uses a TLC plate
2) Paper chromatography – Uses filter paper

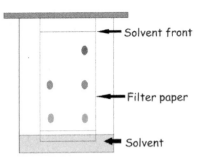

To carry out chromatography:
- Put the solvent into the tank to a depth of 1cm.
- Mark the baseline in pencil (Pen runs!)
- Place a small spot of the sample onto the baseline.
- Place the plate into the tank.
- Take the plate out before the solvent front reached the top of the plate.

We use the R_f value to compare results from chromatography.

R_f = Distance travelled by substance ÷ Distance travelled by solvent

Gas Chromatography

Stationary phase: Silica or alumna powder packed into a metal column.

Mobile phase: Unreactive carrier gas like nitrogen.

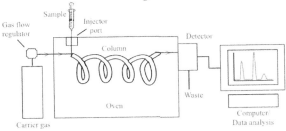

The sample is turned into a gas as it is injected into the column. The carrier gas then pushes this gas through the column.

Different components take different times to travel based on how strongly they are bonded to the stationary phase. The detector sends a signal to the computer as each component leaves the column.

C2.1.7: Purification and Checking Purity

To check if a sample is pure, we can use chromatography.

Thin layer chromatography is better than paper chromatography because:
- Faster
- More sensitive
- Large range of stationary phases and solvents can be used
- Single chromatography spot can be removed for gas chromatography

Gas chromatograms can then be used to analyse samples and compare them.

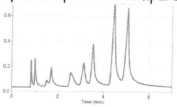

Check Your Understanding

1. Calculate the relative formula mass of glucose, $C_6H_{12}O_6$.

2. Calculate the empirical formula of $C_{24}H_{48}$.

3. Explain how to determine if a substance is pure or impure.

4. Describe how to separate an insoluble solid from a liquid.

5. Describe how to separate a soluble solid from its solution.

6. Describe how to separate two liquids with different boiling points.

7. Explain how chromatography can be used to identify dyes.

C2.2.1: Metals and Non-Metals

Physical Property: Characteristic that can
be observed or measured.

Physical Property	Metals	Non-Metals
Appearance	Shiny	Dull
Melting Point and Boiling Point	Usually high	Usually low
State at room temperature	Solid	Half solid; half gas
Malleable or brittle when solid	Malleable	Brittle
Ductile or non-ductile when solid	Ductile	Non-ductile
Thermal and electrical conductivity	Good Conductors	Poor conductors

Chemical Property: Characteristic that can only be determined by studying its chemical reactions.

Metals lose electrons to form positive ions. Non-metals gain electrons to form negative ions.

Metals and non-metals react with oxygen to form oxides.

If dissolved in water:
Metal oxides produce alkaline solutions
Non-metal oxides produce acidic solutions

When looking at the periodic table, metals are on the left and non-metals are on the right.

C2.2.2: Electronic Structures

Periodic Table of the Elements

H																	He
Li	Be											B	C	N	O	F	Ne
Na	Mg											Al	Si	P	S	Cl	Ar
K	Ca	Sc	Ti	V	Cr	Mn	Fe	Co	Ni	Cu	Zn	Ga	Ge	As	Se	Br	Kr
Rb	Sr	Y	Zr	Nb	Mo	Tc	Ru	Rh	Pd	Ag	Cd	In	Sn	Sb	Te	I	Xe
Cs	Ba	Lu	Hf	Ta	W	Re	Os	Ir	Pt	Au	Hg	Tl	Pb	Bi	Po	At	Rn
Fr	Ra	Lr	Rf	Db	Sg	Bh	Hs	Mt	Ds	Rg	Cn	Uut	Fl	Uup	Lv	Uus	Uuo

La	Ce	Pr	Nd	Pm	Sm	Eu	Gd	Tb	Dy	Ho	Er	Tm	Yb
Ac	Th	Pa	U	Np	Pu	Am	Cm	Bk	Cf	Es	Fm	Md	No

The horizontal rows are called periods.
The vertical columns are called groups.
Elements in a group have similar chemical
properties due to the arrangement of the
electrons.

Electrons are arranged in shells around the
nucleus. The electronic structure shows
how the electrons are arranged in atoms.
The outermost shell of an atom is called
the outer shell.

38

Rules:
1st shell: Maximum of 2 electrons
2nd shell: Maximum of 8 electrons
3rd shell: Maximum of 8 electrons
4th shell: Maximum of 18 electrons

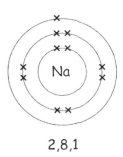

2,8,1

The number of numbers = Period
The last number = Group or the number of
electrons in the outer shell
The sum of the numbers = Atomic number

C2.2.3: Ions and Ionic Compounds

An ion is a charged particle.
Ions are formed when an atom either gains
or loses electron(s).

Metal atoms lose electrons to become
positive ions.
Non-metal atoms gain electrons and
become negative ions.

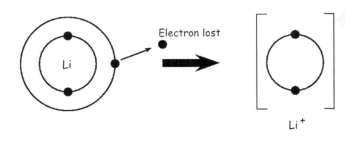

Remember:
If the outer shell becomes empty due to
electron loss, then don't draw it in the ion.
Place square brackets around the diagram.

Include the charge in the top right corner.

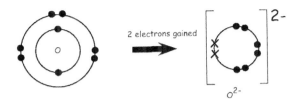

2 electrons gained

O^{2-}

Remember:
Show the gained electrons as the opposite
symbol to the original electrons.
Use square brackets.
Include the charge – Gaining 2 electrons
means 2- charge on the ion.

An ionic bond will form between a metal
and a non-metal.
To draw a diagram to show ionic bonding,
you need to show the electrons from one
ion as dots and the electrons from the
other ion as crosses.

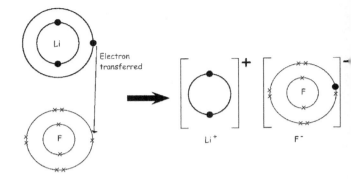

An ionic bond is a strong electrostatic force of attraction between the oppositely charged ions.

Ionic compounds form a giant ionic lattice where the positive and negative ions are in a regular repeating pattern.

C2.2.4: Covalent Bonding

Covalent bonds form between two non-metal atoms.
A covalent bond is a shared pair of electrons.
The covalent bond is a strong electrostatic force of attraction between the nucleus of the bonded atom and the shared pair of electrons.

To draw a diagram to show covalent bonding, we only need to draw the outer shell. The shared electrons go between the two atoms. Remember to still draw one as a dot and the other as a cross.

> *Exam hint: You can work out the number of outer shell electrons by looking at the group number on the periodic table.*

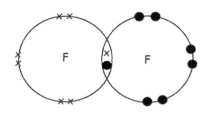

Simple molecules are ones that contain only a few atoms. As these molecules are small, they have weak intermolecular forces so they have low boiling points and tend to be a gas at room temperature. E.g. oxygen

Giant covalent structures consist of many non-metal atoms joined by covalent bonds in a regular repeating pattern. E.g. diamond

Models

We use a range of models to represent atoms and their bonding.

1) Ball and stick models which have the limitation of having exaggerated atom size and bond length. They also suggest the electrons do not move as the model uses rigid bonds.

2) Displayed formulae have the limitation of not showing the 3D shape of the molecule.

C2.2.5: Polymers

A polymer is made from many alkene monomers joining together. To do this they need high pressure and a catalyst.

To name a polymer from the monomer, just add "poly" to the start of the monomer name. E.g. Ethene → Poly(ethene)

To name the monomer from the polymer, take "poly" away from the name. E.g. Poly(styrene) → Styrene

To draw the displayed formula for a polymer:
- Copy the displayed formula for the monomer but change the double bond for a single bond.
- Place brackets around it and extent single bonds out each side.
- Add the letter 'n' to the bottom right corner.

$$\begin{array}{cc} H & H \\ | & | \\ C & = C \\ | & | \\ H & H \end{array} \longrightarrow \left(\begin{array}{cc} H & H \\ | & | \\ -C & -C- \\ | & | \\ H & H \end{array} \right)_n$$

There are two types of polymer:
1) Thermosoftening polymers which do not have cross links between the chains so are easy to separate as the intermolecular forces are easily overcome.

2) Thermosetting polymers which have cross links between the molecules making them harder to separate.

C2.2.6: Structure of Metals

All metals, except mercury, are solid at room temperature. The atoms are arranged in a giant ionic lattice. This means they are arranged in a regular way.

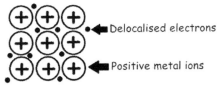

Delocalised electrons

Positive metal ions

Electrons leave the outer shell of the metal atom so it becomes a positive metal ion and the delocalised electrons are free to move through the structure of the metal.

A metallic bond is the strong electrostatic force of attraction between delocalised electrons and positive metal ions.

C2.2.7: The Periodic Table

Dalton
Arranged elements in order of atomic weight and gave each element a symbol.

Newlands
Arranged the elements in order of atomic weight but noticed the properties of every 8th element seemed similar so arranged them into octaves.

Mendeleev
Placed elements in groups based on atomic weight but also placed them into groups based on their properties. He left gaps for undiscovered elements as the properties of the existing elements didn't fit. He also swapped some elements based on their properties.
He was able to predict the properties of the undiscovered elements.

Mosely

Discovered the atomic number was the number of protons in the nucleus. Proving Mendeleev's arrangement was correct.

Ramsay

Discovered unreactive elements like argon and proposed a group to the right of group 7 on Mendeleev's table.

Modern periodic table patterns:
- Arranged in order of atomic number.
- Atomic number is the number of protons in an atom.
- Number of electrons = Number of protons in an atom.
- Group number is the number of electrons in the outer shell.
- Electronic structure determines the chemical properties.

Check Your Understanding

1. Where are metals found on the periodic table?

2. Work out the electronic structure of magnesium.

3. Explain how sodium chloride is bonded.

4. What is a covalent bond?

5. Explain why simple molecules tend to be gases at room temperature.

6. Describe how a polymer is formed.

7. Explain why metals can conduct electricity.

8. Describe how the modern periodic table was created.

C2.3.1: Carbon Allotropes

Carbon is in group 4 and has 4 electrons in its outer shell. It can form 4 covalent bonds.

Allotropes: Different forms of an element in the same state but with different atomic arrangements.

Diamond

Giant covalent structure with each carbon joined to four others.

Diamond has a high melting point and is hard as there are many covalent bonds which require lots of energy to be broken. Diamond does not conduct electricity as all electrons are shared to form covalent bonds so there are no delocalised electrons.

Graphite

Graphite is a giant covalent structure with each carbon bonded to three others. The electron not used in bonding becomes delocalised so graphite can conduct electricity.

Graphite has a high melting point as there are many covalent bonds which require lots of energy to be broken.

Graphite is slippery as the weak forces between the layers are weak and easily overcome.

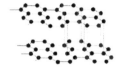

Graphene

Resembles a single layer of graphite. It is extremely strong, conducts electricity and is almost transparent.

Fullerenes

Fullerenes are shaped like tubes or balls.

Nanotubes resemble a sheet of graphene rolled into a tube. They are used to reinforce tennis racquets due to their strength.

A buckyball is 60 carbon atoms arranged in a sphere shape. They have potential uses as lubricants and drug delivery systems.

C2.3.2: Changing State

When a substance changes from a solid to a liquid, some bonds break. When it changes from a liquid to a gas, all remaining bonds break.

The stronger the bond and the greater the number of bonds the greater the energy transferred from the surroundings to break them.

Substances with high melting or boiling points have many strong bonds.

Sublimation: Direct change from solid to gas.
Deposition: Direct change from gas to solid.

C2.3.3: Bulk Properties of Materials

The difference between malleable and brittle substances is to do with how easily the particles can change position in the lattice.

Metals are malleable as the ions can slide over each other and the delocalised electrons are free to move so no bonds are broken.

Giant covalent structures and ionic compounds are brittle are many bonds break simultaneously when a large enough force is applied.

A substance will conduct electricity if it has charged particles that are free to move.

Metals have delocalised electrons so they conduct electricity.

Ionic compounds conduct electricity when molten or dissolved as the ions are free to move. They do not conduct as a solid as the ions are not free to move.

Simple molecules, polymers and giant covalent structures do not conduct electricity as they have no charged particles that are free to move.

Check Your Understanding

1. Define the term allotrope.

2. Name two carbon allotropes.

3. Explain why graphite can conduct electricity.

4. Explain why diamond has a high melting point.

5. Explain what happens when a substance melts.

6. Explain why some materials can conduct electricity.

C3
Chemical
Reactions

C3.1.1: Formulae

Chemical symbols have 1, 2 or 3 letters. The first is a capital and the others are lower case.

Metal formulae are written as the empirical formula as they exist as giant metallic lattices.

Non-metal elements that exist as giant covalent structures are written as their empirical formula.

Group 7 elements exist as diatomic molecules e.g. Cl_2

Molecular formula shows the symbols for each element and how many of each element are present. E.g. H_2O

C3.1.2: Formulae of Ionic Compounds

You can usually work out the charge on a positive ion by looking at the group number.

Hydrogen ions have a +1 charge.
Group 1 ions have a +1 charge.
Group 2 ions have a +2 charge.
Group 3 ions have a +3 charge.

You can work out the charge on a negative ion by subtracting the group number from 8.

Group 7 ions have a -1 charge.
Group 6 ions have a -2 charge.
Group 5 ions have a -3 charge.

Compound ions are ions that contain more than one element. You need to know the following:

Ammonium: NH_4^+
Hydroxide: OH^-
Nitrate: NO_3^-

Carbonate: $CO_3{}^{2-}$
Sulphate: $SO_4{}^{2-}$

When writing ionic formulae, the positive and negative charges must balance.
E.g. Calcium, Ca^{2+}, and Chlorine, Cl^- makes $CaCl_2$.

If a compound ion is present and balancing is required, place brackets around the formula of the compound ion.
E.g. Calcium, Ca^{2+}, and hydroxide ions, OH^- makes $Ca(OH)_2$.

C3.1.3: Conservation of Mass

The law on conservation of mass states that atoms cannot be created or destroyed. In a chemical reaction, they are just re-arranged. This means the total mass of the reactants must be the same as the total mass of the products.

Precipitate: Insoluble solid produced in a reaction involving solutions.

A closed system is a container in which no substance can enter or leave during a reaction.

If you carry out a reaction in a closed system, the mass of the reactants at the start will be the same as the mass of products at the end.

C3.1.4: Chemical Equations

Word equations tell us what the names of the products and reactants are.

Magnesium + Oxygen → Magnesium Oxide

Exam hint: Always write the full names if asked for a word equation or you will lose the mark.

Balanced symbol equations tell us how the atoms are arranged in the reactants and the products and the relative amounts of each substance involved.

To write a balanced symbol equation:
1) Write the symbol equation
2) Count the number of each element on each side of the arrow.
3) Add numbers to the space in front of each formula to balance it.

State symbols show the physical state of the substances in a chemical reaction.

Solid = (s)
Liquid = (l)
Gas = (g)
Aqueous solution = (aq)

C3.1.5: Half Equations and Ionic Equations

Half equations are models for the change that happens to one reactant in a chemical reaction.

E.g. $2Na\ (s) + Cl_2\ (g) \rightarrow 2NaCl\ (s)$

Sodium atoms lose an electron to become Na+ ions:

$$Na \rightarrow Na^+ + e^-$$

Chlorine atoms gain an electron to become chloride ions:

$$Cl_2 + 2e^- \rightarrow 2Cl^-$$

A complete ionic equation shows the ions present in a reaction mixture. It also include formulae of molecular substances or substances in the solid state.

E.g.

$HCl\ (aq) + NaOH\ (aq) \rightarrow NaCl\ (aq) + H_2O\ (l)$

$$H^+ (aq) + Cl^- (aq) + Na^+ (aq) + OH^- (aq) \rightarrow$$
$$Na^+ (aq) + Cl^- (aq) + H_2O (l)$$

As Na^+ and Cl^- are the same on both sides, they are spectator ions. They are not taking part in the reaction.

Net ionic equations leave the spectator ions out:
$$H^+ (aq) + OH^- (aq) \rightarrow H_2O (l)$$

Net ionic equations are used to model precipitation reactions.
This is where an insoluble solid (precipitate) is produced from two solutions.

C3.1.6: The Mole

Mole (mol): Amount of a substance that contains the same number of entities (atoms, ions or molecules) as there are atoms in 12.0g of carbon-12.

Avogadro Constant: Number of entities in one mole, 6.02×10^{23} .

Number of entities = Amount (mol) x Avogadro Constant

Molar mass (g/mol): The mass in grams of one mole of a substance. It is the substances relative atomic or formula mass.

E.g. The molar mass of sucrose, $C_{12}H_{22}O_{11}$:
$(12 \times 12) + (22 \times 1) + (11 \times 16) = 342$g/mol

C3.1.7: Mole Calculations

Mass (g) = Molar Mass (g/mol) x Amount (mol)

To calculate the mass made in a reaction:

1) Work out the molar masses.
2) Rearrange the equation making amount the subject.
3) Substitute in the values to work out the amount made in mol.
4) Look at the balanced symbol equation to work out the ratio of reactant to product.
5) Multiply the ratio up to the number of moles made in step 3.
6) Rearrange the equation making mass the subject.
7) Substitute in and solve.

E.g. Nitrogen reacts with hydrogen to produce ammonia.

$$N_2 \text{ (g)} + 3H_2 \text{ (g)} \rightarrow 2NH_3 \text{ (g)}$$

Calculate the mass of ammonia made from 112.0g of nitrogen.

1) Molar mass of N_2 = 2 x 14 = 28g/mol
   Molar mass of ammonia = 14+(3 x 1) = 17.0g/mol
2) Amount = Mass / Molar Mass
3) Amount = 112.0 / 28.0
          = 4.0mol
4) 1 mol of nitrogen makes 2 mol of ammonia.
5) So 4.0mol nitrogen makes 8.0mol ammonia.
6) Mass = Molar Mass x Amount
7) Mass = 17.0 x 8.0
        = 136g

Excess: Reactant present in a greater amount than that needed to react with the other reactant.

Limiting Reactant: Reactant present in an amount less than that needed to react completely with the other reactant.
The limiting reactant determines the amount of product made.

Stoichiometry: Describes the relative amounts of each substance in a chemical reaction. You can use mole calculations to work out the stoichiometry of an equation.

Check Your Understanding

1. What is the formula of a molecule of chlorine?

2. What is the formula for calcium hydroxide?

3. State the law of conservation of mass.

4. List the four state symbols.

5. What is a spectator ion?

6. Define the term mole.

7. What formula would you use to calculate the mass of a substance when given the molar mass and amount in mol?

8. What is meant by the term limiting reactant?

C3.2.1: Exothermic and Endothermic Reactions

Exothermic: The temperature of the reaction mixture increases. The heat is given out to the surroundings.
E.g. Combustion, neutralisation

Endothermic: The temperature of the reaction mixture decreases. The heat is taken in from the surroundings.
E.g. photosynthesis

Electrolysis and thermal decomposition reactions are endothermic but do not have a temperature decrease. The energy taken in is used to break down substances.

C3.2.2: Reaction Profiles

In a chemical reaction, bonds break in the reactants and then new bonds form between the atoms to make the products.

During a chemical reaction, energy is transferred from the surroundings to break bonds in the reactants to form separate atoms and to the surroundings from the reacting particles when bonds form between atoms.

A reaction profile is a chart that shows the energy involved.

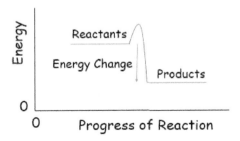

74

Horizontal lines represent the amount of energy stored in the reactants or products.

The energy change is the difference between the energy transferred to break the bonds and the energy transferred to make the new bonds.

Activation energy is the minimum energy needed for a reaction to start.
It is often provided by heating and it breaks the bonds in the reactants.
All reactions have an activation energy.
Sometimes the reactants have enough energy to react and just need mixing. E.g. neutralisation reactions.

Steps to drawing a reaction profile:

1) Draw both axes

2) Draw two horizontal lines, representing the energy stores in the reactants and products.

- Endothermic: Reactant line lower than product line
- Exothermic: Reactant line higher than product line

3) Draw a curve to represent the activation energy.

4) Add labels to your diagram.

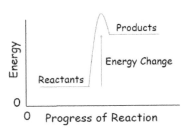

Endothermic reactions: energy transferred to break the bonds is more than the energy transferred when new bonds form.
It is a positive energy change. (Upward arrow)

Exothermic reactions: energy transferred to break the bonds is less than the energy transferred when new bonds form.
It is a negative energy change. (Downward arrow)

C3.2.3: Calculating Energy Changes

Bond energy (kJ/mol): Energy needed to break 1 mol of a particular bond.

Different bonds have different bond energies.

The mean bond energies given in a table used to calculate energy changes may vary from experimental values.

Bond energies can be used to calculate energy changes in a reaction.

You need to use:
- Energy transferred to break the bonds in the reactants
- Energy transferred to make new bonds in the products.

To calculate the energy change:

1) Write down the number of bonds of each type in the reactants.
2) Multiply the number of each bond by the bond energy from the table.
3) Add all these values to give the total energy transferred to break all bonds.
4) Write down the number of bonds of each type in the products.
5) Multiply the number of each bond by the bond energy from the table.
6) Add all these values to give the total energy transferred to make new bonds.
7) Calculate the energy change by using:
   Energy transferred to break bonds
   – Energy transferred to make bonds

Negative sign = Exothermic
Positive sign = Endothermic

Check Your Understanding

1. What is an exothermic reaction?

2. Give an example of an exothermic reaction.

3. What is an endothermic reaction?

4. Give an example of an endothermic reaction.

5. Describe how to draw a reaction profile for an endothermic reaction.

6. What is the activation energy?

7. Explain how to use bond energies to calculate if a reaction is endothermic or exothermic.

C3.3.1: Redox Reactions

Redox reactions are where reduction and oxidation happen at the same time.
Reduction: Loss of oxygen
Oxidation: Gain of oxygen

E.g. Thermite Reaction

Aluminium + Iron (III) Oxide → Aluminium Oxide + Iron
$$2Al \ (s) + Fe_2O_3 \ (s) \rightarrow Al_2O_3 \ (s) + 2Fe \ (l)$$

Aluminium is oxidised as it gains oxygen. It is the reducing agent.
Iron oxide is reduced as it loses oxygen. It is the oxidising agent.
The oxygen is transferred from the iron oxide to the aluminium.

Half equations show the change that happens to one reactant.

$$Al \rightarrow Al^{3+} + 3e^-$$

Aluminium atoms lose three electrons to become aluminium ions. It is oxidised.

$$Fe^{3+} + 3e^- \rightarrow Fe$$

Iron ions gain three electrons to become iron atoms. It is reduced.

Oxidation
Is
Loss of electrons
Reduction
Is
Gain of electrons

Redox reactions do not have to involve oxygen. The reducing agent will lose electrons. The oxidising agent will gain electrons.

C3.3.2: The pH Scale and Neutralisation

Acid
- Release hydrogen ions, H^+ (aq), when dissolved in water to make an aqueous solution.
- pH < 7
- Red, orange, yellow with universal indicator.

Neutral
- pH = 7
- Green with universal indicator.

Alkali
- Bases that can dissolve in water.
- Releases hydroxide ions, OH^-, when dissolved in water.
- pH > 7
- Blue and purple with universal indicator.

Usually pH is measured using universal indicator solution which is added to the test solution and then the colour is identified using the colour chart.

An improved method of measuring pH is using a pH meter:

- Calibrate the pH meter by washing the pH probe with water then place it into the calibration buffer.
- Adjust the reading to match the pH of the buffer solution.
- Wash the probe with water and place in test solution.

Neutralisation: Reaction between an acid and a base, or alkali, to form a salt and water only.

Acid + Base → Salt + Water

Acids contain H^+.
Alkalis contain OH^-.
These react together to form water.
$$H^+ (aq) + OH^- (aq) \rightarrow H_2O (l)$$

The salt is made of the other ions present.
First part = Metal in base/alkali
Second part = From the acid

Acid	Formula	Salt
Hydrochloric Acid	HCl (aq)	Chloride
Sulphuric Acid	H_2SO_4 (aq)	Sulphate
Nitric Acid	HNO_3 (aq)	Nitrate
Phosphoric Acid	H_3PO_4 (aq)	Phosphate

E.g. Sodium hydroxide + Sulphuric Acid $\rightarrow$
Sodium Sulphate + Water

C3.3.3: Reactions of Acids

Carbonates and Acids
Carbonates are ionic compounds that contain the carbonate ion, CO_3^{2-}

Most carbonates are insoluble in water but the exceptions are the group 1 carbonates and ammonium carbonate

Metal Carbonate + Acid → Salt + Water + Carbon Dioxide

To test for carbon dioxide, limewater goes from colourless to cloudy.

Metals and Acids
Metal + Acid → Salt + Hydrogen

To test for hydrogen, a lit splint makes a squeaky pop sound.

PAG C1: Reactivity Trends

Once you have carried out experiments with different metals and acid, you can place them in order of reactivity based on their observed reactions.

To ensure you obtain valid results, you should only change the metal being reacted and repeat the experiment to identify anomalies. All other variables should be controlled e.g. temperature, concentration of acid etc.

You can identify the more reactive metals as they will release gas bubbles faster.

C3.3.4: Hydrogen Ions and pH

A solution is a solute dissolved in a solvent. The greater the amount of solute it contains, the greater the concentration.

Dilute acid contains a low ratio of acid to volume of solution.
Concentrated acid contains a high ratio of acid to volume of solution.

Acids release hydrogen ions in aqueous solution. The covalent bond breaks between hydrogen and the other part of the substance to form the hydrogen ion and the negative ion.

The strength of an acid is determined by how many hydrogen ions are released or how ionised it is.

Weak acids are partially ionised. This means only some of the hydrogen ions are released from the molecule.
Strong acids are fully ionised. This means all of the molecules release their hydrogen ions.

$\rightleftharpoons$ means reversible. The reaction with this arrow does not go to completion so will be a weak acid.

When the concentration of H^+ ions increases by a factor of 10, the pH of the solution decreases by 1.

A pH titration curve shows the effect on pH of changing the hydrogen ion concentration during a neutralisation reaction.

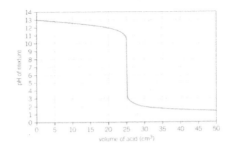

1. Measure 25cm³ of dilute alkali and place in beaker.
2. Estimate pH using universal indicator or pH meter.
3. Add 1cm³ of dilute acid, stir and record the pH.
4. Repeat until you have added an excess of acid.
5. Plot results on a graph.

Check Your Understanding

1. Explain what is meant by the term reduction.

2. Explain what is meant by the term oxidation.

3. What do half equations show?

4. Describe how to test the pH of a substance.

5. Name the salt made in the neutralisation of nitric acid with sodium hydroxide.

6. What is the general word equation for the reaction of an acid and carbonate?

7. Explain the difference between concentration and strength of acids.

91

C3.4.1: Electrolysis of Molten Salts

Electrolysis: Process in which an electrical current is passed through a compound causing a chemical change.

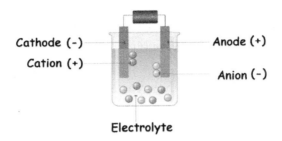

Cathode (-) Anode (+)
Cation (+)
Anion (-)

Electrolyte

- Two electrodes (metal or graphite) that conduct electricity to the electrolyte.
- Electrolyte (compound in liquid state or solution) – Contains mobile ions and conducts electricity.
- Electrical supply (Power pack)

Cathode: Negative electrode
Anode: Positive electrode

Cation: Positive ion
Anion: Negative ion

Positive ions gain electrons at the cathode to become atoms.
Negative ions lose electrons at the anode to become atoms.

A binary ionic compound contains just two elements. E.g. Lead bromide, $PbBr_2$ (l)

Cathode produces lead: $Pb^{2+} + 2e^- \rightarrow Pb$
Anode produces bromine: $2Br^- \rightarrow Br_2 + 2e^-$

Ions are discharged when they become atoms or molecules.

As the ions close to the electrodes are discharged, the concentration of ions by the electrode decreases.

Other ions move to replace them by diffusion and convection. This can't happen when ionic compounds are solid.

C3.4.2: Electrolysis of Solutions

Electrodes are usually made from inert (unreactive) materials such as copper, platinum or graphite as they remain unchanged during electrolysis.

Electrolysis of Water

Water is partially ionised.
It has small concentrations of hydrogen and hydroxide ions.

$$H_2O \ (l) \rightleftharpoons H^+ \ (aq) + OH^- \ (aq)$$

Reduction at cathode:
$$4H^+ \ (aq) + 4e^- \rightarrow 2H_2 \ (g)$$

Oxidation at anode:
$$4OH^- \ (aq) \rightarrow 2H_2O \ (l) + O_2 \ (g) + 4e^-$$

Electrolysis of Solutions

Aqueous solutions contain ions from dissolved ionic compounds. It will contain hydrogen ions and hydroxide ions from water. This leads to competition at the electrode as only one ion is discharged at each electrode.

Hydrogen is produced at the cathode unless ions from a less reactive metal are present, in which case that metal is produced.

Oxygen is produced at the anode unless ions from an element in group 7 are present at a high enough concentration, in which case the group 7 element is produced instead.

PAG C2: Electrolysis

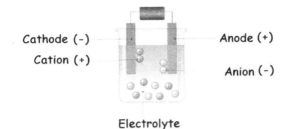

Cathode (-)   Anode (+)

Cation (+)   Anion (-)

Electrolyte

The anode will be connected to the positive terminal of the power pack. The cathode will be connected to the negative terminal of the power pack.

You can collect the gas products from each electrode using small test tubes to allow you to test them later.

If nothing happens when you turn on the power supply, there are three checks to do:

1) Ensure each electrode is under the surface of the electrolyte.
2) Make sure all connections are secure.
3) Replace each piece of apparatus in turn (e.g. for faulty wires)

The three gas tests you may need to use with electrolysis:

Hydrogen – Lit splint makes a squeaky pop

Oxygen – Glowing split relights

Chlorine – Damp blue litmus paper turns red then white.

C3.4.3: Electroplating

Electroplating uses non-inert electrodes (they change during electrolysis.)

In electroplating:
- Cathode: Object you want to coat
- Anode: Metal you want to coat the object with
- Electrolyte: Solution containing ions of the coating metal.

Metal ions from the electrolyte are discharged on the surface of the object. Metal ions leave the anode to replace the discharged metal ions. Eventually the anode is used up.

Silver atoms lose electrons at the anode:
$$Ag\ (s) \rightarrow Ag^+\ (aq) + e^-$$

Silver ions gain electrons at the cathode:
$$Ag^+\ (aq) + e^- \rightarrow Ag\ (s)$$

Silver ions move through the electrolyte.

Electrons move through the wires between the two electrodes.

Purifying Copper

Extracted copper is not pure so it doesn't conduct electricity as well as pure copper. Copper is purified using electrolysis.

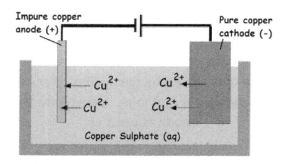

Anode: Impure copper
Cathode: Pure copper
Copper (II) Sulphate solution: Electrolyte

Cathode gains copper atoms and increases in mass.

Anode loses copper atoms and decreases in mass.

Impurities from the anode collect underneath is (sludge).

Check Your Understanding

1. What is the name of the positive electrode in electrolysis?

2. What is the name of the negative electrode in electrolysis?

3. Explain the process of electrolysis.

4. During the electrolysis of water, what will form at the anode and what will form at the cathode?

5. During the electrolysis of potassium bromide solution what will form at the anode and what will form at the cathode?

6. Explain how to electroplate a ring with silver.

About Wright Science

Wright Science is a YouTube channel created by Vicki Wright, a secondary science teacher in England.

I started Wright Science as a resource for my own classes to have extra help outside of school time. It started with a single recap video for each exam back in 2013 and then just grew. These days there are videos for every lesson on both the separate science courses and combined science courses which are used by a number of students across the country and world!

I hope that you find this book useful and welcome your comments.

Good luck in your exams!